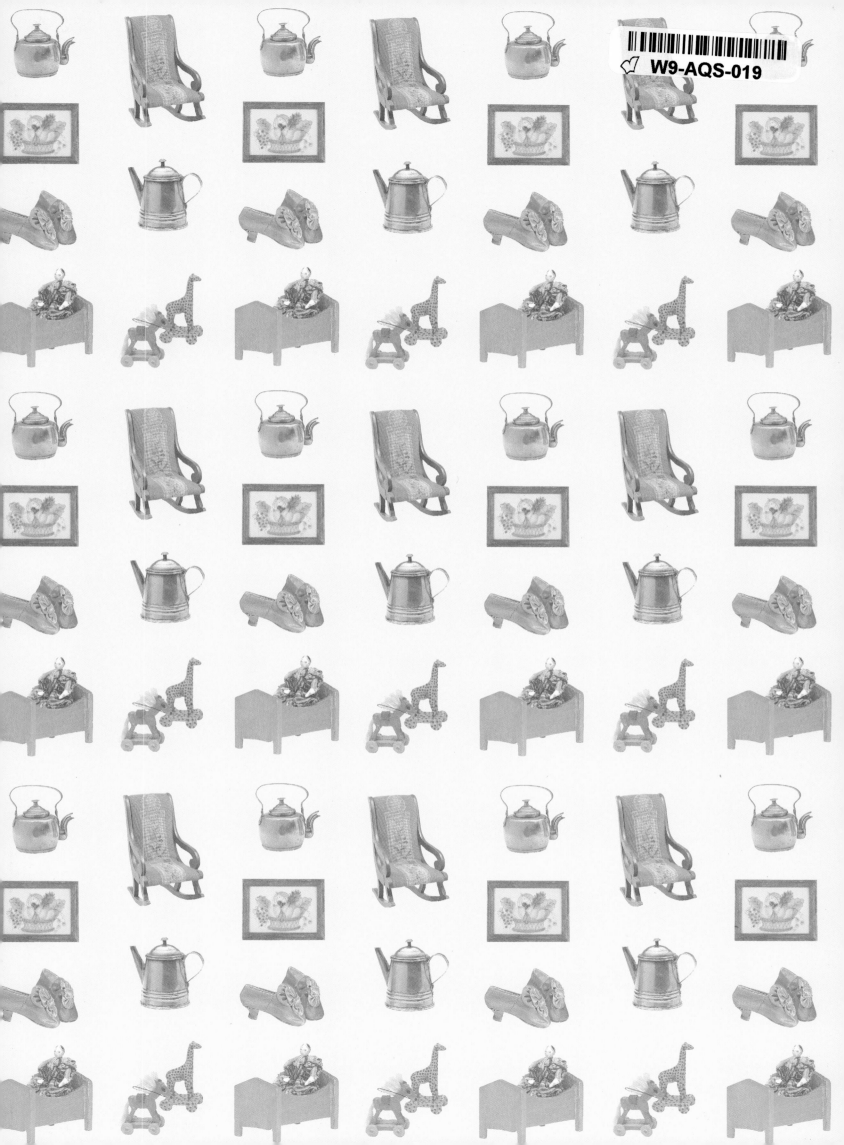

DOLLHOUSES
MINIATURE KITCHENS
AND SHOPS

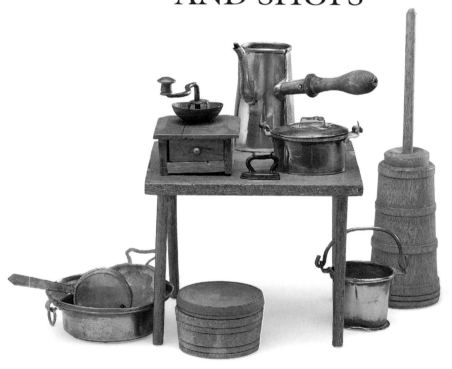

From the Abby Aldrich Rockefeller Folk Art Center

DOLLHOUSES
MINIATURE KITCHENS AND SHOPS

By Susan Hight Rountree

Photography by Tom Green

Additional photography by David M. Doody and
the staff of the Colonial Williamsburg Foundation

The Colonial Williamsburg Foundation
Williamsburg, Virginia

Library of Congress Cataloging-in-Publication Data

Abby Aldrich Rockefeller Folk Art Center.
    Dollhouses, miniature kitchens, and shops from the Abby Aldrich
Rockefeller Folk Art Center / by Susan Hight Rountree ; photography by
Tom Green ; additional photography by David M. Doody and the staff of
the Colonial Williamsburg Foundation.
        p.   cm.
    ISBN 0-87935-159-4
    1. Dollhouses. 2. Doll kitchens. 3. Miniature retail stores. 4. Minia-
ture objects—Virginia—Williamsburg. 5. Abby Aldrich Rockefeller Folk
Art Center. I. Rountree, Susan Hight. II. Title.
NK4892.U6W563 1996
688.7'23'0747554252—dc20   95-36507
                                                  CIP

This book was designed by Helen Mageras.

Printed and bound in Canada.

Foreword

The Abby Aldrich Rockefeller Folk Art Center at Colonial Williamsburg is known primarily for its outstanding collection of American folk art. Of the large number of paintings purchased in the 1920s through early 1940s by the collection's founder, Abby Aldrich Rockefeller (Mrs. John D. Rockefeller, Jr.), a significant number feature children ranging from infants to teenagers. Some of these pictures also show children with playthings, including hoops and sticks, carts, hobbyhorses, and more often dolls and doll-size furniture that parallel early toys now also in the museum's collection. The toy holdings at the Folk Art Center have grown rapidly in recent years, due largely to two significant bequests and many other gifts from friends. The toy collection comprises a second important body of material culture that teaches and informs us about family life, education, and childhood play among early Americans.

Since the museum's founding in 1957, staff at the Folk Art Center have mounted an annual holiday exhibit featuring the toys. Without question, this display of German, American, and English playthings is a highlight of the season for visitors. Few items in the show exceed in popularity the two dollhouses featured in this book. Both are exceptional and rare examples of their kind, distinctive for their periods of manufacture, and very different in design and furnishings. Together they provide a rare glimpse of nineteenth- and early twentieth-century Americans' fascination with the domestic world made small. They were expensive and sophisticated toys on a grand scale, owned originally by families of considerable means. The great variety of arrangements and make-believe vignettes owners could affect in these miniaturized households by simply moving items about or adding and deleting others was a large part of the fascination dollhouses held for their young (as well as older) mistresses and masters.

The extraordinary history and documentation surviving for the Morris-Canby-Rumford dollhouse provide an excellent story of how such toys were cherished and played with over many generations. The house, a miniaturized version of a Philadelphia town dwelling of the period, was made by Caspar Wistar Morris (1764–1828) for his twin daughters, Elizabeth Clifford Morris and Sarah Wistar Morris, born in 1813. Sarah died only a few years after the house was made and thus her sister Elizabeth inherited it and subsequently passed it on to her daughter Elizabeth Morris Canby (1848–1933), who married Charles Grubb Rumford. The Rumfords' oldest son, Samuel Canby Rumford, inherited the house from his mother. Samuel and his wife, Mary Beatrix Tyson Rumford, had one son who survived into adulthood, Lewis Rumford II. There were no little girls in these two generations and the dollhouse saw limited use from about 1875 to the third decade of the twentieth century, although throughout these years it was carefully preserved and was regarded by each successive owner as a cherished part of family history.

Elizabeth Clifford Morris Canby, the surviving twin who originally owned the dollhouse, is shown here with her daughter Elizabeth Morris Canby, who inherited the house. Taken from a daguerreotype of about 1857 owned by the family.

According to family history, the Morris-Canby-Rumford dollhouse remained in Samuel Rumford's house in Wilmington, Delaware, until 1951. It was here that Samuel Rumford fabricated a number of miniature reproductions of early American furniture that also had passed down through the family. His wife, Mary Beatrix Tyson Rumford, assisted him with upholstery work for some of the pieces and later his daughter-in-law, Rose Rumford, added the miniatures of extant family portraits. The oldest of Lewis Rumford II's daughters, Beatrix, recalls that an invitation from her grandparents to play with the house was special and usually occurred during the quiet afternoon hours, when the senior members of the family took very long naps.

The three daughters of Lewis II and Rose Rumford, who played with the dollhouse in the l940s-1950s, after it was refurbished for them by their grandfather Samuel C. Rumford. From the left are Beatrix Tyson Rumford, Ellen Ellsworth Rumford, and Elizabeth Clymer Rumford.

In 1951 the house moved to Lewis II and Rose Rumford's Baltimore residence. All of their children—Beatrix, Ellen, Elizabeth, and Lewis III—fondly remember playing with the dollhouse, although as the youngest and as a boy, Lewis III admits he was sometimes elbowed aside!

The five oldest of Lewis and Rose's grandchildren were the last of the family children to play with the house in Baltimore before it was given to the Folk Art Center in l981. It seemed important to the Folk Art Center staff that the children of Lewis III, all of whom were born well after the dollhouse came to Williamsburg, also be given an opportunity to touch and experience the small world of this now-famous family treasure. Some of the eighteenth- and nineteenth-century family furniture miniaturized for the dollhouse by their great-grandfather adorns their own home. Julia, Grace, and Will are shown on page 3 during their day with the dollhouse in Williamsburg. During the course of a photography session with the children playing with the house, Will, who is the youngest, was nudged aside by his sisters! History does seem to repeat itself.

Independent of the important documented history of the Morris-Canby-Rumford dollhouse are the ideas about early childhood and education that nineteenth-century toys embodied. Not all families could afford elaborate dollhouses; more could afford to purchase a "room" or setting such as the imported Nuremberg kitchens and other shop interiors featured in this book. Many more could afford inexpensive German wooden toys, including miniaturized versions of villages, farms, market scenes, armies of soldiers, and Noah's arks. The great majority of toys, made both in Europe for export and in America, were small replicas of larger real-world objects, events, or activities. They were meant to delight and instruct by directing a child's imagination to useful, real-life tasks. As Sue Rountree so clearly points out in her text, early manufacturers stressed the importance of instruction afforded by such toys.

Regardless of century, the make-believe world of children is often a mimed perception of adult activities. Toys of the kind discussed here enhanced a child's ability to learn about grownup behaviors and duties at a formative age. Keeping house, food preparation and service, biblical stories with strong moralistic messages, the transactions of going to or operating retail shops and markets, and learning the names of the accoutrements and utensils associated with a shop or kitchen were vital lessons learned at play. Children could spend hours in these activities without ever repeating imagined scenarios and becoming bored. There were countless ways of controlling and ordering the small, intricate environments, and these settings provided the mechanism for children quietly to play out ambitions, disappointments, and other emotions as they occurred or might occur in their young lives.

Toys of this kind seem as remarkable and interesting to us today as they did to their original owners. It is a great pleasure to realize the publication of this book, which discusses in detail the two dollhouses and related miniaturized settings owned by the Folk Art Center. For many years, visitors to the museum have asked for such a book; they have been patient and tireless in their encouragement, as have those on the staff, who also saw the need to provide more in-depth information on the houses, their histories, and their furnishings. Several persons contributed significantly to the project, foremost among them Sue Rountree, whose knowledge of miniatures and dollhouses and whose skill as a miniature craftsperson are well known. Additionally, Sue has for years led the team of museum volunteers who annually install the houses for the Folk Art Center holiday exhibit; she has also been a significant contributor to the Long Island dollhouse.

Anne Motley, Folk Art Center registrar, also provided considerable assistance with the logistics necessary for a project of this sort. Anne's intimate knowledge of the furnishings and her years of experience in inventorying and accounting for the incredible number of "smalls" contained in the houses has been a rewarding, though arduous, job. Appreciation and much admiration is extended to Tom Green for his superb photography of the houses, the settings and interiors, and the delicate small objects. He has captured the essence of these miniatures, so much so that they seem life-size, as they might have to young owners. Suzanne Coffman, associate editor, and Helen Mageras, senior graphic/book designer, have dedicated many hours to this project, resulting in a meticulously prepared and handsomely presented publication.

There have been numerous donors to the Folk Art Center's toy collection over the years, including the gift of the Morris-Canby-Rumford dollhouse, and two large bequests from the estates of Effie Thixton Arthur and Mrs. Roy E. Tomlinson. Many items from the latter are illustrated in this book. To these donors as well as those of individual items that have been presented over the years, a special note of gratitude is extended.

Carolyn J. Weekley
Director, Abby Aldrich Rockefeller Folk Art Center

Preface

Ah! The Doll's house! . . . open, there were three distinct rooms in it: a sitting-room and bedroom, elegantly furnished, and, best of all, a kitchen, with uncommonly soft fire-irons, a plentiful assortment of diminutive utensils—oh, the warming-pan!—and a tin man-cook in profile, who was always going to fry two fish. What Barmecide justice have I done to the noble feasts wherein the set of wooden platters figured, each with its own peculiar delicacy, as a ham or turkey, glued tight on to it, and garnished with something green, which I recollect as moss! Could all the Temperance Societies of these later days, united, give me such a tea-drinking as I have had through the means of yonder little set of blue crockery.

> Charles Dickens, "A Christmas Tree," published in *Household Words,*
> December 21, 1850

There is nothing as fascinating as a dollhouse, little kitchen, or toy shop for those of us who love small things. Just as Dickens remembered how he enjoyed tea in "yonder little set of blue crockery" during his childhood in early nineteenth-century England, we, too, find ourselves instantly drawn into the fantasy world of make-believe. People have always been intrigued by the large made small. From ancient Egypt, Phoenicia, and Rome, little models of rooms and shops remain for us to see. Miniatures continued to be popular and collecting them was fashionable throughout the seventeenth and eighteenth centuries. During this period large and extravagant European "baby houses" or "cabinet houses" were built and furnished not for children but for the amusement of wealthy adults.

By the early nineteenth century, nearly every child wished to have a dollhouse, small toy kitchen, or miniature shop. The dollhouses that remain from this period in the United States were probably constructed by local cabinetmakers or family members. The smaller toy kitchens and shops, however, were imported in great numbers and were available furnished and unfurnished in a variety of styles and prices. The majority of

The Carl P. Stirn catalog of 1893 advertised an impressive-looking dollhouse covered with lithographed paper. Several firms were mass-producing less expensive dollhouses.

these miniature rooms came from Germany until the mid-nineteenth century, when Dutch, English, and French products also became available. At this same time, a number of toy companies along the East Coast of the United States began making their own toys in addition to importing European playthings. The dollhouses and small rooms were intended not only to entertain but also to teach a child how to organize and manage a home, kitchen, shop—or even a post office! These toy structures remained popular throughout the century, and a great many of them have survived.

A puzzle advertised about 1840 in the toy catalog of the Sonneberg firm of Louis and Edward Lindner shows a group of children playing with a toy kitchen.

A page from a Nuremberg pattern book of 1850–1860 shows a colorful array of painted turned woodenware that would have delighted any child furnishing a dollhouse or goods shop.

Miniatures continue to be immensely popular today. Enthusiasts travel widely to visit well-known dollhouses and miniature collections. All are interesting for both their workmanship and what they reflect about the times in which they were created.

The Folk Art Center collection includes two remarkable dollhouses, the Morris-Canby-Rumford dollhouse, a compact and handsome early nineteenth-century cabinet dollhouse, and the Long Island dollhouse, an impressive, 12-foot-long, Colonial Revival-style structure believed to have been built in Long Island, New York, about a century later. In addition to the dollhouses, the Folk Art Center has a collection of toy kitchens and miniature shops, all shown filled with appropriate furnishings and accessories.

These structures and their furnishings present some interesting puzzles. Who made them? Who played with them? Who added certain pieces to them, and when? Wherever possible, we have tried to answer or suggest answers to these questions. Unless the history of a particular piece has been recorded, we must rely on information from catalogs, prints, other accounts, and makers' marks. The Folk Art Center library includes several toy catalogs published from 1803 into the twentieth century. They are invaluable, but in the end, without specific documentation for a piece or structure, we can only suppose what might have been.

These houses, kitchens, and shops and their Lilliputian furnishings all show the wear and additions of many generations. We hope they will evoke happy memories from your childhood and add pleasure to an adult hobby.

The many kitchens and shops available offered a child tantalizing choices. Imagine the excitement of receiving this basket shop (from the Nuremburg pattern book of 1850–1860) stocked with such a variety of baskets and even a cradle on rockers!

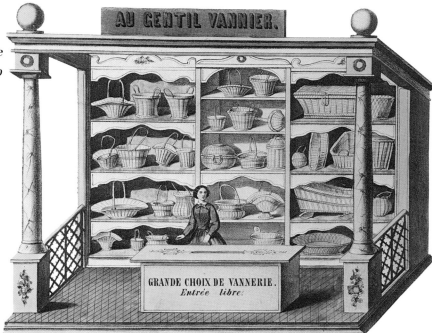

AU GENTIL VANNIER.

GRANDE CHOIX DE VANNERIE.
Entrée libre.

The Morris-Canby-Rumford Dollhouse

With its doors closed, this imposing structure is 53¹/₂ inches tall,
40 inches wide, and 21¹/₂ inches deep. It is painted to resemble
a two-story brick dwelling, possibly similar to the Morris family's
Philadelphia home.

Four equally spacious rooms are revealed when the doors are open. It is not hard to imagine the young Morris girls enjoying their new house.

This rare and extremely well pre-served early nineteenth-century Philadelphia dollhouse is the remarkable product of a family whose members planned, built, and furnished it around 1820 for twin sisters, Sarah Wistar Morris and Elizabeth Clifford Morris. It is even more remarkable that much of the furniture original to the house still exists.

In 1981 the dollhouse and its contents were donated to the Folk Art Center at Colonial Williamsburg by Mr. and Mrs. Lewis Rumford II. It has become a focal point of the Folk Art Center's Christmas exhibit, where it is enjoyed by many visitors each year. When the dollhouse was being readied for its move, two paper la-bels were discovered on the back. Written in Elizabeth Morris Canby's hand, the labels identify her grandfather, Caspar Wistar Morris, as the maker of the doll-house in 1820.

The dollhouse was built of yellow pine and poplar in a manner reminiscent of European "baby houses" or "cabinet houses," with two hinged doors that open like a cupboard to reveal four rooms. The high ceilings allowed and encouraged the children to rearrange and play with the furnishings. The exterior, except for the glazed windows on one side, is painted. The fine quality of the painting suggests that Caspar Wistar Morris may have hired a local decorative painter to do this work.

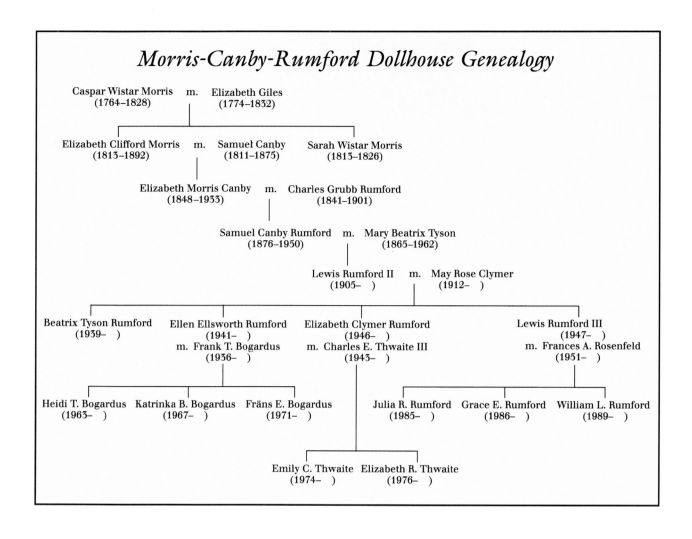

Morris-Canby-Rumford Dollhouse Genealogy

Caspar Wistar Morris m. Elizabeth Giles
(1764–1828) (1774–1832)

Elizabeth Clifford Morris m. Samuel Canby   Sarah Wistar Morris
(1813–1892)   (1811–1875)   (1813–1826)

Elizabeth Morris Canby m. Charles Grubb Rumford
(1848–1933)   (1841–1901)

Samuel Canby Rumford m. Mary Beatrix Tyson
(1876–1950)   (1865–1962)

Lewis Rumford II m. May Rose Clymer
(1905–)   (1912–)

Beatrix Tyson Rumford   Ellen Ellsworth Rumford   Elizabeth Clymer Rumford   Lewis Rumford III
(1939–)   (1941–)   (1946–)   (1947–)
                         m. Frank T. Bogardus   m. Charles E. Thwaite III   m. Frances A. Rosenfeld
                         (1936–)   (1943–)   (1951–)

Heidi T. Bogardus Katrinka B. Bogardus Fräns E. Bogardus   Julia R. Rumford Grace E. Rumford William L. Rumford
(1963–)   (1967–)   (1971–)   (1985–)   (1986–)   (1989–)

Emily C. Thwaite Elizabeth R. Thwaite
(1974–)   (1976–)

The windows on the first floor facade are shuttered. Stone lintels suggesting English basement windows are included. The fanlight above the door and the large fan in the pedimented roof are nicely detailed, as are the bricks, recalling other eighteenth- and nineteenth-century English and American cabinet houses. The corner blocks, windows, and large fan are typical features of the 1820s. The turned feet, survivals from a nineteenth-century table, were added by Samuel Canby Rumford, a family descendant, in 1939. They protect the painted surface of the lower front and sides of the house.

A number of the original furnishings in the house survives. Because of the Morris family's metropolitan location and the quality of the miniatures, it is possible that these early pieces, all in the Empire style so popular at the time, were made by a craftsman in the Philadelphia area. Other closely related items with the same shallow crosshatched carvings and glass knobs have been seen in miniature collections from the area. Another possible source for the dollhouse's fashionable items might have been the firm of Adrian Forst, which was established in Philadelphia in 1817 and advertised both domestic and imported miniature furnishings. Later pieces may have been purchased for Elizabeth Morris Canby from the Philadelphia Toy Manufacturing Company, which was in business by 1838.

In 1939, Samuel Canby Rumford created many additional items for his grand-children, who had inherited the dollhouse. These miniature pieces were based on full-size antique furniture that continues to be owned by the family. Rumford carefully drew the designs to scale on paper before he constructed his small copies. Later, three generations of family needleworkers reupholstered pieces, created fabric-covered cardboard chairs, made bed hangings, crocheted rugs, and fabricated period costumes for the dolls. During this same period, people outside of the family gave gifts to the house, including the tiny doll in the cradle, which has a recorded purchase date of 1825. These artifacts provide a glimpse of those who shared in the life of this house—for surely to a child a dollhouse does have a life that is as active and exciting as the children who play with it.

American dollhouses of this quality and early date are extremely rare. Even rarer is an example like this one, which survives with complete documentation of its ownership over many generations. The Morris-Canby-Rumford dollhouse reflects the love and attention lavished on it over the years. Each object, whether original to the house in the 1820s, added in the 1850s, copied from a family heirloom in 1939, or given by a family friend or others interested in the dollhouse, has a particular history. Collectively, the furnishings are a rich visual record of one family's continual care and preservation of an important material aspect of each generation's childhood.

The youngest Rumford generation—Grace, Julia, and William—enjoy the family dollhouse.

This walnut tall case clock, made and signed by Samuel Canby Rumford in 1939, was based on an eighteenth-century clock made in Philadelphia for an ancestor. Manufactured with English works, the full-size clock is still in the family. Family members tell how Samuel Canby Rumford found a broken watch while out walking one day and decided it would make a "fine face" for his miniature clock.

Dining Room Much of the dining room furniture is original to the house and was probably purchased for it about 1820. The then-fashionable Empire stand and the sideboard with their glass drawer knobs, the tilt-top table, and the dining table have similar crosshatch designs near their bases.

Samuel Canby Rumford, the great-grandfather of the children shown on page 3, made the clock and the six chairs at the table. He also made the corner cupboard filled with a set of tableware made in the 1870s by Irish workers in a Trenton, New Jersey, ceramics factory known for its Beleek porcelain and white graniteware. His wife stitched the silk chair seats.

The window cornices and false-grained fireplace have always been in the house, as have such small items as the little gilded white cup and saucer in the style of Paris porcelain seen on the Empire stand on the right. The gilt and porcelain vase on the mantel is in a style popular in the 1840s and 1850s. Other items, some antique, were added in the 1950s.

The daguerreotype is of Sarah Wistar Morris, one of the two little girls for whom the house was made. She died in 1826 at the age of thirteen, and the house therefore descended through the line of her twin sister, Elizabeth.

On the table is some miniature German glass, the gift of a friend. A closer view of the chairs shows the stitched silk seat cushions. Also on the table, a turkey is ready for the holiday festivities. The pewter salt stand and pepper caster were purchased by a family member on her first trip to Williamsburg in the 1950s.

Most of the original knobs, made from cut-glass beads, are still in place on the Empire stand and sideboard. Notice the similar cross-hatching designs on each piece. Irish cut-glass decanters, which are original to the house, flank a pewter tea service. A tiny copper teapot formed from a U. S. penny—its "ONE CENT" shows clearly on the bottom and reveals its origin—sits on the brass tray.

Kitchen

Colorful pottery and glass are housed in the tall built-in cupboard. The cupboard, smoke-grained fireplace, large worktable (on the bottom of which "S. W. Morris table" appears to be written in pencil), and many of the copper pots and pans either came with the house or were added very early in its history. The 1939 oilcloth floor covering lends a cheerful note. A variety of shapes and sizes of turned wooden buckets, scoops, and other essential accessories for such an early kitchen are found in this room. Most were probably imported from Germany and sold in Pennsylvania stores.

Most of the copper pots and pans, the bucket and side-pouring copper coffeepot, the working coffee mill, the turned wooden pail and butter churn, and the flatiron are original furnishings.

The old iron pot hanging on the fireplace arm is ready for soup or stew making. An early tinplate Dutch oven—a reflecting oven with a roasting spit—stands in front of a 1940s bell that is disguised as a doll. On the mantel over the fireplace are a large red tole tray with red and green hand-painted flowers on a gold ground, a mottled brown and green glazed vase and cup, glass baluster candlesticks, and a mantel clock. The wooden butter churn beside the fireplace is another necessary utensil for an early nineteenth-century dollhouse kitchen.

This well-organized kitchen has one of three fireplaces in the house. A tall cupboard fixed to the wall holds a large quantity of glass and pottery. The smallest jug on the lowest shelf of the cupboard has the delicate mottling of Beleek wares and was probably part of a gift to the family.

A blue and white transfer-printed earthenware platter is similar to one inscribed "Hackwood" for a firm working in Hanley, England, in the Staffordshire area between 1827 and 1843. It was part of a toy dinner service belonging to Elizabeth Morris Canby. A white bowl with a blue design, a slip-decorated earthenware pitcher, and a stoneware bottle with a handle are but a few examples of the pottery and porcelain assembled in the house.

Two dolls, a peg-wooden doll from the 1820s seated in the window and another from more than a century later, converse under family portraits while sitting on furniture crafted by members of the family.

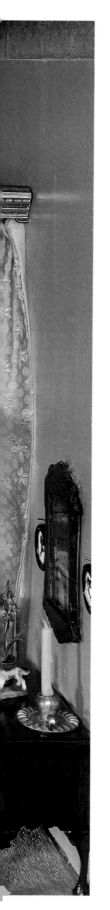

Parlor This room holds a number of the miniatures Samuel Canby Rumford made for the house in 1939 and 1940, including a dressing table, a looking glass, a sofa, footstools, a cherry desk, and a Windsor chair. He based each piece on eighteenth-century furniture that had descended in the family and he signed each miniature. About the same time, other family members crafted the two upholstered chairs and dressed the dolls. The needlepoint rug, whippets, and late nineteenth-century Austrian bronze flowers came from a family friend. The room has been restored to its original ocher color with a gilt paper border at the ceiling. Other unrestored rooms in the house have paper borders, although they are currently obscured by modern layers of paint. A family member recounted how the pendulum on the mantel clock always moved because the family home vibrated, thus making the dollhouse come alive to a little boy.

The cherry desk is based on an eighteenth-century Pennsylvania family piece. The secondary wood used in the working drawers is cedar salvaged from cigar boxes by Samuel Canby Rumford. Little cubbyholes provide ample space for correspondence. A small drawer could be the hiding place for the tiniest of treasures. A miniature book titled Plaisir et Gâité, *printed in Paris in 1837, is beautifully bound in leather with gilt edging. A wastebasket made from a small metal pill container decorated with a map of the world is a later generation's addition.*

Two walnut Windsor chairs made by Samuel Canby Rumford are reproductions of early family pieces. On the left is a rocking chair used in the bedroom; on the right, a chair copied from his wife's desk chair.

11

Three miniature portraits of family members hang on the back wall of the parlor. The largest likeness is of Samuel Canby, who married Elizabeth Clifford Morris, one of the girls for whom the dollhouse was made. Her portrait and that of her father-in-law, James Canby (1781–1850) are appropriately placed in daguerreotype frames.

At the back of the room is a drop-leaf table with the crosshatched design found on pieces in the dining room and bedroom. A small hand-painted porcelain figurine of a lady with a parrot is placed on a stand next to an arrangement of flowers.

A page from the pattern book of toys offered by the Sonneberg firm of Louis and Edward Lindner around 1840 shows a later style of peg-wooden doll. The joint construction is nearly the same, but the 1820s doll in the dollhouse has a hair comb, high-waisted dress, and painted "bobbed" hair with translucent black curls framing her face, characteristic of the early 1820s. After 1840, the waistline was lowered and the hair combs were eliminated.

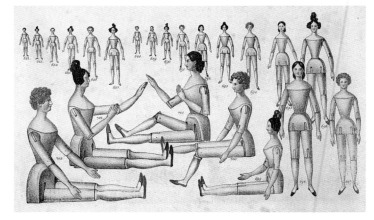

An early peg-wooden doll with a finely detailed face, known to the family as the "Old Lady Doll," sits with her pet whippet on a plush sofa. The doll is original to the house. The "tucked comb" style dates her to the early 1820s. Overhead is a caged celluloid parrot that was given to the family in the 1940s, about the same time that the footstools, upholstered chairs, and sofa were re-covered.

Bedroom A late nineteenth-century china-headed doll perches on the edge of the bed, dressed by a grandmother and granddaughter in the family during the 1940s. The grandmother, Mary Rumford, also crocheted the rug and made the chintz bed hangings. The wooden cradle next to the doll holds a tiny peg-wooden doll, 1 inch in length, purchased in 1825. This petite doll is jointed at the shoulders, elbows, hips, and knees, as is the peg-wooden doll on the parlor sofa. The smaller doll and its cradle were gifts in the 1940s from a stranger who read a newspaper article about the dollhouse and wrote, "You may wonder . . . why I offer the doll to a stranger. . . . it's obvious that you cherish it [the dollhouse] and would care for the wooden doll too. . . . she has been cherished for so long I feel an absurd sense of responsibility for her." An 1850s toleware box added by Elizabeth Morris Canby sits at the foot of the bed.

An assortment of objects resides on the top of the dressing table, which is very similar to the piece in the parlor. The gilt-edged ceramic clock dates from the earliest days of the house. One wonders if the two tiny beaded dolls were a gift to the twins for whom the house was made.

A finely detailed wooden carving represents the best craftsmanship of mid-nineteenth-century German carvers. Standing next to it is a metal-winged angel from the 1950s who wears a rather dubious expression.

The walnut dresser is typical of the Empire style fashionable in the early nineteenth century. The dresser retains all but one of its original glass knobs—tiny glass beads nailed onto the drawer front.

A marvelously detailed late nineteenth-century bronze rabbit holding a clover sits next to a colorful modern oriental bowl that is inscribed "Japan" and imitative of cloisonné work.

Two nineteenth-century china-headed dolls visit with a pet poodle. Perhaps the child on the bed is talking to the tiny jointed doll in the cradle beside her.

Interesting furniture in this room based on family heirlooms includes the chest-on-chest, rocking chair, looking glass, and dressing table. The four-post bed in the style of the 1840s was added for Elizabeth Morris Canby. The bureau was part of the orginal furnishings.

A neatly cross-stitched "C," for Canby, and the blanket-stitched edging are part of a set of hand-sewn bed linens that also include the pleated bedspread, pillows, and hangings.

This fashionable 1840s four-post bed and the tole painted chest must have been enjoyed by Elizabeth Morris Canby.
A china-headed doll sits on the bed beside another doll in its cradle.

A remarkable survivor from the mid-nineteenth century is the tin potty-chair painted to imitate wood grain, a popular decorative technique. Early nineteenth-century records survive showing several German firms, the best-known being Rock and Graner, who exported large quantities of metal furnishings painted in this fashion to the United States. The potty-chair even has its original potty, which may be retrieved by lifting the metal flap seen at the back. The piece was added for Elizabeth Morris Canby, who would have played with it in the 1850s.

Copy of Chest on Chest made in Philadelphia by Thomas Affleck 1775 for David Deshler.

S.C. Rumford 1939.

This chest-on-chest was copied by Samuel Canby Rumford in 1939 from a full-size family treasure that was commissioned in 1775 by Rumford's ancestor David Deshler as a wedding gift for Deshler's daughter Catherine. Notice the inscription on the back of the miniature and the cigar-box wood used in the drawer. The full-size original chest (shown above) is now exhibited in the Selected Masterworks Gallery at Colonial Williamsburg's DeWitt Wallace Decorative Arts Gallery.

This is a house of truly grand proportions—over 12 feet long, 6 feet high, and 3½ feet deep. The rooms are made up of a series of boxes of different depths that form the structure when assembled. The back is unfinished and, because the rooms are not uniform in depth, the back surface is uneven. Thus the house was made to be viewed from three finished sides. Exterior design features of note are the third floor and roof areas as well as the clapboarded left end of the house, which shows both the French doors from the parlor and the bay window in the bedroom above. A balustrade outlines the roof area over the kitchen. To the right of the kitchen is a freestanding toolshed.

This unusually large dollhouse was first shown to visitors to the Folk Art Center during the 1969 Christmas season. It had been acquired less than a year before by the well-known toy company F.A.O. Schwarz in New York, which exhibited it briefly before the dollhouse came to Colonial Williamsburg.

Unfortunately, very little is known of the dollhouse's history. A contractor discovered it in 1968 in the attic of a Long Island mansion he was demolishing. He never revealed either the mansion's location or its owner.

The house came to Williamsburg sparsely equipped with furniture and accessories in a variety of sizes, as might be expected of a dollhouse of this size that may have spanned several generations. Many of the objects are from the nineteenth century; others are early twentieth-century pieces. In 1971 an anonymous donor gave a number of items that have added immensely to the "lived-in" quality of the house. Somehow everything coexists successfully in this splendid house.

Among the furniture, paintings, rugs, and objects added to the house over the years by individual donors are a stenciled floorcloth, marzipan foods, overmantel paintings, needlepoint rugs, and bed hangings. Contemporary miniatures of furniture, paintings, and theorems in the Folk

Long Island Dollhouse

Art Center's collection also help furnish the rooms. Some antique items, such as a handsome brass and crystal chandelier that hangs in the entrance hall, have been given to the Folk Art Center to use in the house. In addition, the staff and volunteers who ready the house for exhibition each Christmas have become the next generation to carry on the traditions of the dollhouse. Their care and attention add a greater dimension to the life of this house.

Visitors are frequently heard to say that they "could step right inside and feel at home" in this house. Built primarily of plywood, its layout and most of the interior and exterior architectural features are in the Colonial Revival style and date the house to the early twentieth century. Especially noteworthy are the interior details. Arched keystoned doorways with paneled sliding doors connect the front rooms, and three different styles of doorways lead us from the front rooms into the ones behind. Other interesting details include a grand arched fireplace alcove, wide crown molding, extensive wall paneling, a long bay window with upholstered seat, and scribed random-width flooring anchored with minuscule pegs. Visitors who peek into the side rooms will find another bedroom, a fully equipped kitchen, and a separate toolshed. The unusual layout and the painstaking architectural details suggest that elements in this dollhouse might have been modeled after those in a real house.

Two items found in the dollhouse offer tantalizing clues about its former owners: a towel embroidered with the letter "B" and a tiny alphabet sampler with the initials "H.A.B." and the date "1876" stitched at the bottom. What a pity the contractor did not reveal enough information to give us more details of what must have been the remarkable history of this enchanting house.

This small cross-stitch sampler measuring 5¹/₂ inches tall by 5¹/₈ inches wide was worked in crimson red wool on 14-count Penelope canvas.

Imagine an 11-inch-tall Victorian-style chair, typical of mid-nineteenth-century Empire furniture, with wooden arms and needlepoint upholstery; a 7¹/₂-inch tall Windsor rocking chair with a diamond-shaped inlay in the back rail; an elegant early nineteenth-century neoclassic side chair measuring 5¹/₂ inches tall; and a 4¹/₈-inch tall Shaker rocking chair made according to today's standard 1:12 scale, all in the same house.

Today most miniatures have a one inch to one foot ratio. Thus this 4¹/₈-inch-tall Shaker rocker represents a chair that was about 50 inches tall. Not all miniatures in this house, however, follow this scale. Certainly the 11-inch chair was not modeled after one that was 11 feet tall.

When examined closely, a pair of ivory Stanhope binoculars, or "peepers," reveals the inscription "Ice Mt. Niagra Falls" on one side and "General Views: Niagra Falls—six views, Made in France," on the other. Stanhopes were popular souvenirs that usually pictured tourist attractions, historical figures, or religious subjects such as the Lord's Prayer.

Notice the fine details of the paneling and the working pocket doors on both doorways. The scribed floors are in correct scale with the stair treads and other architectural features.

Front Hall

The downstairs hall provides a grand entrance with its impressive staircase decorated with Christmas greens. The tall settle, table with a pierced base, gold-decorated table, binoculars, and umbrella are all found in photographs taken when the house was owned by F.A.O. Schwarz. A contemporary needlepoint rug was added after the house was acquired by the Folk Art Center, as was the 1840 brass and crystal chandelier that is possibly of French origin.

A finely detailed Waltershausen table with gilt transfer decoration was made in Germany, probably in the mid-1860s. The carpetbag fashioned from nineteenth-century paisley material, the inquisitive kitten, and a flower arrangement in an acorn cap are more recent additions.

Parlor The parlor, one of the most
spacious rooms in the house, is filled with
pieces that exhibit fine craftsmanship. The
large scale of the furniture, much of which
came with the house, is appropriate con-
sidering the 18-inch-high ceilings.

A former Colonial Williamsburg pastry chef made many of the foods for the dollhouse, including this marzipan fruit in a porcelain bowl.

These three books are typical of volumes that would have been in Victorian homes. The Gift of Piety is inscribed "Master I. L. Waterman, June 1851."

A finely crafted Empire sofa, 16 inches long and inlaid with figured wood, provides a comfortable spot for an 1810s peg-wooden doll to play with her cat and doll while admiring the Christmas tree. A male doll, dating about 1890, stands on a needlepoint rug beside his book, Dew Drops, and a magnifying glass. Perhaps he is about to enjoy some of the fruit on the antique marble-top table, which probably dates to the nineteenth century. On another early nineteenth-century table behind the sofa (see detail) are a pair of brass candlesticks and a painted wire basket holding fresh greens.

The sofa's fine inlay and splendidly carved paw feet surmounted by acanthus leaves typify the fine craftsmanship seen on many pieces in the house, as does the handsome burl veneer used for the curved legs and angled surface of the tabletop.

An impressive carved fireplace with a faux marble base is hung with stockings awaiting Santa's visit. The brass fire tools, porcelain clock, and matching vases came with the house when it was acquired in 1969. In the background a large tree is surrounded with presents—a Noah's ark (based on nineteenth-century German arks), a pile of blocks, a fishing pole, and a toy elephant. The tree decorations are miniatures of ones on the always-popular Christmas tree at the Folk Art Center.

Below: *An assortment of nineteenth-century bisque and glazed china figurines is displayed on a four-tiered corner étagère.*

In a corner of the parlor two chairs, one upholstered with floral needlework upholstery and the other with a silk cushion of floral design, are placed beside a large, circular tripod tea table covered with books and a dried flower arrangement. A looking glass with elaborately carved fretwork hangs above the table. The French doors that lead into the room are visible on the right. The braided rug on the floor is one of several old rugs in the house.

A cabinet and hanging shelves filled with books flank one side of the room and a tall case clock faces the room and the inlaid table in the center. These furnishings appear in the photographs taken after F.A.O. Schwarz acquired the house from the contractor.

Game Room

Visitors can look through this finely paneled game room into another room behind. The arched doorway with its keystone and detailed molding above the curve and the post-and-lintel doorway leading to the room to the right, the pocket doors, and the openings on either side of the door to the back are all elements of the popular Colonial Revival style. It is interesting to note the stained plywood that was used throughout the house. Note also the plywood floors, which have been scribed and pegged in a random-width pattern.

Although its pendulum and one weight are missing, this 11-inch-high clock is still impressive. The turned columns support a top that, like the base, has incised gold designs, perhaps to replicate inlay. On the back are the penciled letters "WKLI[?]," which may be the initials of the maker or the original owner.

A skillfully inlaid tilt-top table on a wide pedestal base is placed on a painted floorcloth—a new addition to the house. The two chairs and the table are original to the house. The china-headed doll dates from the 1890s.

Little details always make a difference in furnishing a home of any size. Here a pipe and well-worn playing cards suggest that our gentleman will enjoy a game of cards and a smoke.

This 11-inch-tall two-drawer secretary with mirrored doors is filled with an interesting collection of books given to the Folk Art Center by an anonymous donor in 1971. The eleven copies of Dew Drops, a collection of daily readings from the Bible, are identical except for their bindings. Some are dated 1889, whereas others are undated. Other books include the Life of General Tom Thumb (1889), Gift of Piety (1851), Dot's Travels (1874), and a Bible inscribed "Bought of a little boy in Philadelphia for Frank Herbert by his father March 1856." A tripod stool with spool legs is upholstered with floral needlepoint and trimmed with gold fringe.

A glimpse of the back of this desk reveals a hand-beveled panel. The classic Victorian scrolled foot is also seen on many pieces of furniture in the house. The letters "Sd/Cmd" are visible on the back.

This stately room with its chandelier and tables and chests set with china, glass, silver, and an abundance of food provides much to see. A place mat is used as a rug under the table, which gives an idea of the size of this room.

Dining Room
The dining room is a large paneled room 40¼ inches wide by 29¼ inches deep. It is pleasingly furnished with chairs, tables, and chests of varying scales. A post-and-lintel doorway with a sliding door leads into the hall. An arched doorway and a much smaller post-and-lintel doorway open into back rooms. The corner fireplace is lined with blue and white tiles.

Two cupboards hold china, and a number of pieces of china and glass are placed on the ledge encircling the room. A fully laden dining table is in the center of the room; a set of eight neoclassic chairs is arranged against the walls.

Sets of milk glass decorated with tiny roses resembling fine bone china were popular in the late nineteenth century. They were produced by a number of manufacturers, but the best-known sets were made in Thuringia, Germany, and exported to Europe, England, and the United States.

The white glazed dishes, made of a heavier clay, also are decorated with tiny roses and gold bands. No marks are present to help identify this pattern or the maker.

33

A large painting of Carter's Grove, the eighteenth-century seat of the Burwell family located on the James River, hangs over a corner fireplace lined with hand-painted delft tiles. Next to the fireplace is a colorful and detailed theorem painting hung above a nineteenth-century metal tiered plate stand that holds a variety of china and pottery. Urn-shaped knife boxes and a covered ceramic bowl are placed on the mantel. An elaborate set of silver Dutch hearth tools and a brass bucket occupy the other side of the fireplace. The knife boxes, Dutch hearth set, and some of the china were the gift of an anonymous donor in 1971.

An insightful miniature portrait of George Washington was based on an 1865 reverse oil painting on glass by William Matthew Prior, who was greatly influenced by Gilbert Stuart. Ruben Law Reed's 1885 painting of Washington and Lafayette at the Battle of Yorktown was the inspiration for this meticulously executed 2-inch scale work. Both full-size works are in the Folk Art Center.

A late nineteenth-century china-headed doll stands as hostess before a table that holds a marzipan cornucopia, turkey, and bread. An eighteenth-century carving set and other pieces of silver and china complete the setting.

The marzipan cornucopia overflowing with fruit was made especially for this table by Colonial Williamsburg's pastry chef in 1978.

The miniature silver tea set, made in Chester, England, in 1913, bears the maker's mark "CS*FS" for the firm of Saunders and Shepherd. A pair of unmarked plated silver candlesticks, an unmarked silver urn, a knife and fork with carved details on their handles, and an ornate filigreed carving set add to the elegance of the table.

Red Bedroom

The large four-post bed (15 inches in height) with its red-printed bedcover, matching curtains, and window-seat cushion dominates this setting. Much of the furniture in this room came with the house. Notice how small the desk is compared to the large washstand and bed. Despite the differences in scale, we are drawn into this cheerful room.

Beautifully made silk pumps with tiny metal buckles are marked "M.G." and reveal fine handiwork. The composition heels are painted to match the fabric.

This closely woven straw hat of unknown date is decorated with red silk flowers—the envy of any lady.

A sturdy leather-covered trunk ($3^7/_8$ inches high by $7^1/_2$ inches wide by $3^7/_8$ inches deep) is bound with black leather strips that are held in place with roundheaded brass nails. The sheet-iron hinged lock and the brass lock plate are highly detailed, like many full-size ones.

Some of the most skillfully crafted pieces of furniture and accessories in the house are found in this room. The elegantly turned bedposts and all of the construction details are similar to those found on a comparably made full-size bed. The washstand is fitted with a complete set of bathing wares, even a sponge and a toothbrush holder. The room's pale yellow walls emphasize the deep cornice and paneling.

A late nineteenth-century bronze cat listens intently to the activities of some mice in the next room.

One of a series of hand-colored prints in pressed metal frames recalls the illustrations featured in popular nineteenth-century fashion magazines such as Godey's Lady's Book. *A skillfully painted contemporary miniature of* Baby in Red Chair, *one of the most beloved paintings in the Folk Art Center collection, represents a very different style.*

The large (7³⁄₄ inches tall by 9¹⁄₈ inches wide) walnut bureau is well made and well supplied with accessories. Among the latter are several sizes of ivory bristle brushes and combs, a chamber stick and candle, a pierced ceramic dish, a paper-covered box for trinkets, and an adjustable brass mirror. The profile of the scrolled feet and curved stiles on the front, typical of early Victorian styles, are similar to those on several other pieces in the house.

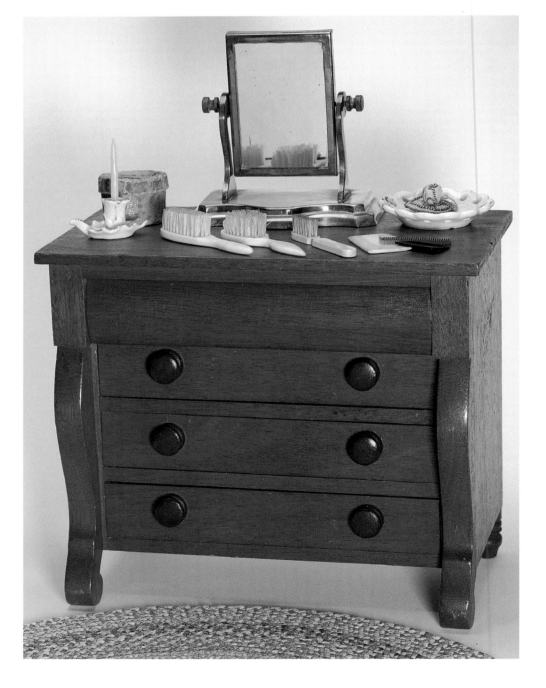

An unmarked doll with a composition head is very similar to ones made by Ludwig Greiner of Philadelphia between 1840 and 1858, after which his dolls carried his patent label. Her molded and painted wavy hair is pulled back from her face and her facial features are delicately painted. These details and the joints of her carved wooden lower arms and legs, which are covered with paper bands, are similar to those on dolls made in the 1830s in Sonneberg, the center of the German doll industry during this period. The doll was the gift of an anonymous donor in 1971. She is dressed in green gauze and black lace accented with red silk ribbon and trim over several petticoats and pantaloons. Her hand rests on a gilded desk. An inkpot with a tiny quill pen stands ready to use. A neoclassic chair is upholstered in red silk and a basket of mending is close by.

Music Room In this paneled room, whose corner fireplace is similar to the one in the dining room, hand-blown bottles and pottery are displayed along the ledge above the paneling. A painting from the 1970s of a nineteenth-century clipper ship hangs over the mantel. The wooden spinet and swivel stool with painted floral decorations were made by the well-known Tynietoy company in Providence, Rhode Island, between 1928 and 1940. The hinged top of the spinet folds down over the painted keys. A rolltop desk in the far right corner is conveniently located near the crank phone on the wall.

Tiny hand-cut stencils were used to create this colorful miniature theorem based on one in the Folk Art Center.

As in the dining room, decorative paneling has been applied to the stained plywood walls, but here dentil molding was added under the ledge holding the glass and pottery. Unlike the dining room, the upper portion of the walls is painted light blue with white trim.

A set of hand-painted arrow-back chairs forms a semi-circle around a music stand and a collection of instruments are ready for an impromptu performance. The cradle bench matches the chairs. Refreshments are waiting on the scalloped-edge low table. The fringed needlework rug with a floral design is a lively reminder of nineteenth-century tastes.

41

These 1:12-scale miniatures include objects and toys from the Folk Art Center collection.

Upper Hallway

This deep, narrow hallway had few furnishings in it when the house arrived in Williamsburg; only the ornate wooden brackets with the bisque figures were present. It is always a temptation to fill an unused space in a doll-house. The Tynietoy settee, the Shaker rocker, and the natural-colored Windsor chair, although not new, were added in the 1970s. The two large paintings were done about that time also. The rest of the furniture and toys, except for the quilting frame, are all contemporary miniatures of objects in the Folk Art Center collection.

Several toys are based on objects in the Folk Art Center's collection. The fleece-covered lamb and painted rooster have movable wheels.

43

This painted poplar chest from Wythe County, Virginia, was made between 1810 and 1825. Three panels display stylized tulips in vases in rust, cream, and black. A recent conservation study found that the replacement feet on the chest were incorrect, so they have been replaced with simple bracket feet. The miniature chest in the foreground has sheet-iron strap hinges and a till, both present on the original chest.

This full-size painted cat is carved from a block of wood with a tail and metal ears added. His quizzical expression has amused visitors over the years. The miniature cat sits on the 1:12-scale chest and seems equally pleased with himself.

A paper label inside this old colorful dome-lidded box indicates that it belonged to Sylvia A. Sherman in 1830. It was made in New England or New York state by an unidentified craftsman. The miniature in the foreground has the same rolled-wire hinges and painted design as those on the original box.

A worn painted New England cupboard is based on a late seventeenth-century example in Colonial Williamsburg's collection. Of particular note are the large reverse-S hinges. Colonial Williamsburg's reproduction pewter mugs line a shelf.

This small chest was made between 1725 and 1750, possibly by Robert Crossman of Taunton, Massachusetts. It is white pine and has a distinctive vine springing from a wavy line and includes C-curves, dots, and leaves.

This full-size nineteenth-century wooden hatbox was made by an unidentified craftsman. The modern miniature below has a similar crosshatch design on the sides and popular weeping willow design on the top.

Each of these pieces of furniture—and even the cat—is a 1:12-scale miniature of an object in the Folk Art Center collection. The "Sutton Fireboard," based on an original made in 1820, is typical of many fireboards designed and painted with receding depth and a highly stylized vase of flowers. A seven-spindle American Windsor chair and a simple ladder-back chair with woven seat are placed on either side of a small tapered-leg tavern table. All suggest the wear visible on the full-size pieces. The small dark brown chest with the worn vine design and cotter-pin hinges is based on the original made in Taunton, Massachusetts, shown above.

White Bedroom This room,

like the others, exhibits some unusual architectural details. The ledge encircling the room intersects with and functions as the capital on each column. The columns support a similarly detailed arch with a keystone. The arch outlines a recessed alcove containing a paneled fireplace. A much smaller doorway leads to the upper hallway on the left.

A wallpaper-covered box with leather-strap hinges has a yellow ocher background with designs of white leaves, burnt sienna dots and veins, and a brown leaf design in the center. It is lined with newsprint from The Eagle, *no. XI. Careful inspection reveals a portion of "An Address to the Clergy of New England." A signature in ink reads, "Elizabeth Gleys—Sandwich, Mass."*

The 16-inch-tall canopy bed does not overpower the small early nineteenth-century peg-wooden dolls who have gathered to play. Recently painted miniatures of folk art paintings lend a charming touch to the walls.

This alcove, unusual in a dollhouse, with its numerous Colonial Revival features makes us wonder if the builder was including details from a real house. The three grooves in the columns, archway, and keystone lighten what could have been an awkward and heavy feature.

47

An early peg-wooden doll, made in Germany about 1810, wears a high-waisted dress and a carved comb in her hair. She tends the baby in the wooden-wheeled woven basket carriage. A nineteenth-century rocking horse whose loosely pinned front legs move back and forth can be seen behind the painted metal miniatures of Schoenhut circus figures balancing on a chair and a barrel. A tiny multijointed peg-wooden doll emerges from her egg-shaped holder. Notice the handworked lace, fine pleating, and embroidered cutwork in the bed hangings.

This canopy bed has elegantly turned posts, a splendid headboard and footboard, and even carving and caning hidden beneath the mattress and bedding. The bed hangings are modern but, with the exception of the scalloped skirt, are made from late nineteenth-century petticoat fabrics and laces. The pillows are made from old handkerchiefs. The small, unmarked ironstone chamber pot has a blue and gold design with red berries and is believed to have come with the house.

Green Bedroom The third bedroom in the house, with its unusual paneling on the left-hand wall, is located above the kitchen. Permanent window cornices with horizontal panels above are featured over the two windows. An ample room, this bedroom is filled with interesting cast-iron and wooden furnishings, some handcrafted, others manufactured.

The heavy-looking rope bed with acorn finials is covered with a silk patchwork quilt made recently from antique fabrics. A mirror, brush, and hat are at home on a green-painted bureau. Nearby is a rocking chair with inlay on the back rail. Also displayed on the back wall is a cast-iron bureau.

On this painted washstand hangs one of the tantalizing clues to the origin of this dollhouse: a linen towel embroidered with the letter "B." It is known to have come with the house's furnishings. A ceramic pitcher and bowl, a bone toothbrush and its holder, a waste bucket, and a soap dish are ready for their small owner.

A pair of red needlepoint slippers with tiny green and yellow designs are neatly placed beside the bed.

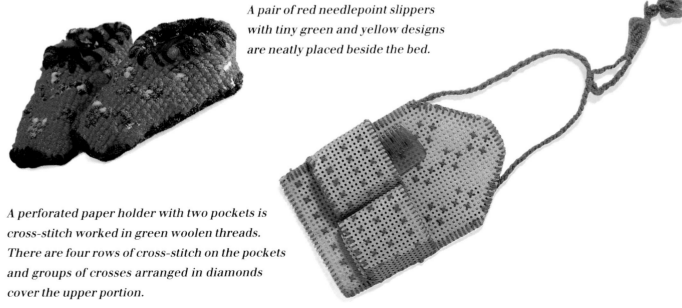

A perforated paper holder with two pockets is cross-stitch worked in green woolen threads. There are four rows of cross-stitch on the pockets and groups of crosses arranged in diamonds cover the upper portion.

A number of firms produced filigree cast-iron toy furniture. One of the largest, S. S. Stevens (later Stevens and Brown, then J. & E. Stevens) of Connecticut, advertised a cradle and bureau in its 1868, 1872, and 1883 catalogs that are similar to those in the dollhouse. The openwork cradle often used in this room is painted navy blue and red with gold stenciling on the solid front panel. The bureau is pierced in a diamond lattice design with a floral or heart-shaped design on each drawer front. It is painted a yellowish brown with a cream-colored top. The drawer pulls, center design, and top edges are painted scarlet red. Miniature cast-iron furniture of this type was produced in large quantities in the mid- to late nineteenth century, although it was never as popular as wooden furniture. (1872 and 1883 catalogs donated for reproduction by Inez B. McClintock.)

An unidentified artist's theorem painting on velvet from about 1825 with its airy, free, and imaginative composition influenced this delicate little miniature.

A handcrafted rocking chair with diamond-shaped light wood inlay along the top rail has nicely shaped arms and seat. At 7½ inches high and 5 inches wide, it is one of many pieces of this size that coexist with much larger and some smaller furniture.

These japanned, or painted, tinplate containers with labels for tea, sugar, and semolina were produced—often in several languages—by various German manufacturers. After 1840 mass-production techniques enabled large quantities of such kitchenware to be produced and exported from Germany. Two of these examples are labeled in French, the third in German.

Herbs hang to dry in bunches from the ceiling, copper pans glisten, and there is much activity at the table and stove. The red-painted cast-iron "Arcade 721" table (made in Illinois in the late 1920s by the Arcade Manufacturing Company) on the left is covered with salad makings; nearby shelves contain pewter plates. A cast-iron model "A-1" stove has four burners, a side grill, and an oven.

Kitchen One of the favorite rooms in a dollhouse is the kitchen, a room that always stimulates a child's imagination. Many items are needed to furnish it and more can always be added.

Here in this kitchen filled with every imaginable kind of utensil, there is ample opportunity to arrange and rearrange the pans, copper molds, pewter plates, baskets of breads and fruits, and decorated plates and pitchers. Some items, such as the pump at the sink or the meat grinder, actually work. Many manufacturers of full-size kitchen equipment also made miniature versions of their stoves, grinders, pumps, and even ice cream machines.

A working cast-iron pump enabled water to be pumped into the sink from a pail or cistern beneath it.

The intricately made black silk doll bears a remarkable similarity to a very skillfully made rag doll from Brazil that was possibly fabricated as late as 1930. The two dolls' costumes, jewelry, shoes, facial and other features—including heavy, pendulous arms—and use of celluloid pieces for fingernails are nearly identical. The doll stands before a cast-iron meat grinder and appears to be busy fixing a meal for the family. This grinder is made exactly like a full-size one. Baskets of fruits and vegetables stand nearby. Perhaps a new batch of bread is being prepared in the large bowl on the table.

The doll presides over an "A-1" cast-iron stove. Numerous copper molds and other implements hang on the wall behind it. Pots filled with foods are cooking on the stove, and a loaf of bread has just been taken from the oven to cool. A cat is oblivious to the little mouse peeking from beside the broom.

A crispy loaf of bread fresh from the oven cools in its tin baking pan. Tiny crocheted mitts protected the hands that removed it.

A wooden egg rack was a popular addition to a nineteenth-century doll's kitchen. This is a typical example with turned legs and two layers that hold a dozen eggs each.

A late nineteenth-century painted bronze cat enjoys its bowl of food by the warmth of the stove.

This handmade doll of black silk is solidly stuffed with cotton. The elbows, knees, hips, and other details are sewn into the body. Black curly hair is sewn onto the head, glass eyes have been inserted, and the eyebrows and mouth have been stitched using very fine stitches. Tiny pieces of translucent celluloid material have been inserted for fingernails. The doll's costume exhibits more of the same fine needlework and includes a white linen blouse with crocheted trim at the neck and sleeves, a silk fichu over the blouse, a skirt gathered in tiers, and a silk bandanna around her head. Delicately made silk shoes are sewn onto her feet. She wears glass beads around her neck, has gold bead earrings, and a gold bead is sewn onto one of her fingers.

Turned woodenware painted to look like china was first made in south Germany for export around 1825. It continued to be manufactured in great quantities throughout the century. A copper colander, pitcher, and large container are stored in the bottom of the cupboard. A basket filled with bread, another of apples, and a butter churn are nearby.

A blue design finely painted on a yellow ground gives the effect of delicate china but is actually the work of German wood turners. These sets were sold in wood boxes and were shown in pattern books such as the beautifully hand-colored page to the left from the catalog of toys offered by the Sonneberg firm of Louis and Edward Lindner around 1840.

A hodgepodge of saws, cleavers, hammers, and axes as well as kettles and crockery fill this little shed.

Toolshed The freestanding toolshed is one of the remarkable and unusual features of this dollhouse. It is filled with wonderful examples of what one might expect to find in such a building. Many handcrafted tools, some broken as can be expected, a revolving grindstone, sawhorses, lanterns, crockery, a wire pen with poultry, and even a yoke for oxen are stored here.

Handcrafted saws, planes, a hammer, and a wrench all could be put to good use. Note the detailed handles on the two saws.

In 1803 Bestelmeier advertised this kitchen as a "new style of toy kitchen" that was "much more natural than current models. . . it has a roof with a chimney, two glass windows, and a wall which extends." It permitted a "neat and tidy arrangement," and a box was available "to pack it away in." The dishes were purchased separately.

An illustration from Paul Hildebrandt's The Toy in the Child's Life (Das Spielzeug Im Leben des Kindes) (Berlin, 1904), shows two little eighteenth-century girls "cooking" on an open hearth that would have been similar to their mother's stove and to the Bestelmeier example.

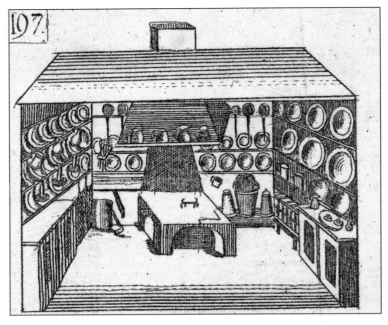

A large collection of tools and kitchen utensils is shown on a hand-colored page from the toy catalog of the Sonneberg firm of Louis and Edward Lindner from about 1840. What a thrill for a child to receive any one of these boxes filled with "useful" goods to add to an already crowded kitchen or shop.

Kitchens and Shops

Toy kitchens and shops were especially popular in Germany in the eighteenth and nineteenth centuries. By the beginning of the nineteenth century, the Nuremberg dealer Georg Hieronimus Bestelmeier had already included them in several catalogs. In his edition of 1803, he showed three kitchens in what we call the "Nuremberg" style as well as numerous shops and a wide variety of other items "for the Educational and Pleasant entertainment of Youth." Bestelmeier's selections were for those who wanted to "enjoy themselves but also want to learn."

The most popular toy room was the kitchen, which closely mirrored the full-size kitchens of South Germany. German toy kitchens remained a favorite into the twentieth century, long after this type of kitchen ceased to exist in children's homes. Many parents approved of their children's playing with toy kitchens because they wanted their offspring to learn to run a happy and efficient household, which at that time centered around the kitchen.

Children, always fascinated with small mechanical items, must have been delighted by coffee roasters and grinders, pumps, fruit squeezers, ice cream machines, and meat grinders, all of which had handles that turned and compartments that opened. Many of the pumps worked, and

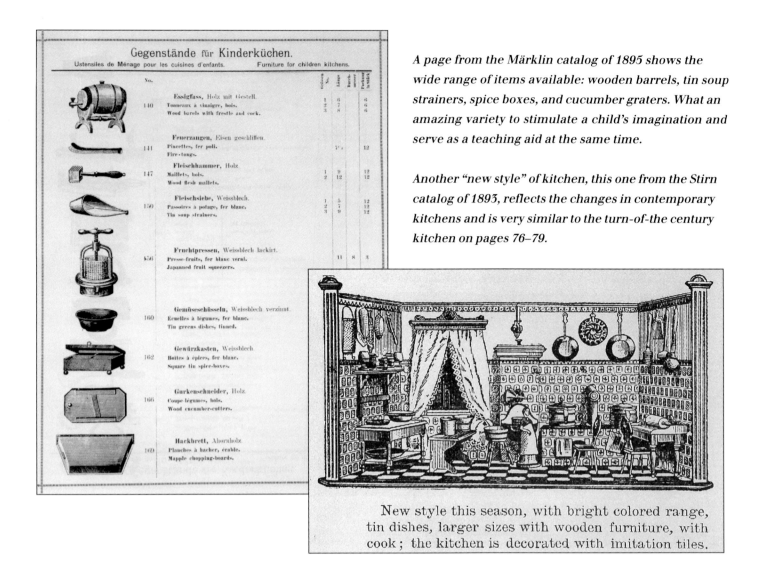

A page from the Märklin catalog of 1895 shows the wide range of items available: wooden barrels, tin soup strainers, spice boxes, and cucumber graters. What an amazing variety to stimulate a child's imagination and serve as a teaching aid at the same time.

Another "new style" of kitchen, this one from the Stirn catalog of 1893, reflects the changes in contemporary kitchens and is very similar to the turn-of-the century kitchen on pages 76–79.

New style this season, with bright colored range, tin dishes, larger sizes with wooden furniture, with cook; the kitchen is decorated with imitation tiles.

the meat grinders could "grind" soft bits of oatmeal, a popular ingredient for "cold cooking."

German firms produced many different toy shops by the early nineteenth century, and Dutch and English manufacturers also were making them well before the middle of the century. Each miniature business was stocked with every conceivable item needed for a particular kind of shop.

Children have always imitated adults and enjoyed pretending they were going shopping or were shopkeepers serving customers. Whether the setting was a dry goods store, a grocery, a butcher's shop, or a millinery shop, children were able to imi-

tate what they saw in real life. Items needed to be weighed, measured, or packaged for the "customer," and bills of sale had to be prepared. Parents encouraged this play and the skills it taught their children. As the 1803 Bestelmeier catalog stated, toy shops were "useful things for instruction and pleasant activities of the young."

The Folk Art Center has three toy kitchens, two shops, and a post office. All are thought to date from the nineteenth century and all show much evidence of being used and enjoyed. We can imagine how these toys mirrored their young owners' lives and the delight they provided while each child played in a world in miniature.

This "play kitchen" from the 1803 Bestelmeier catalog came with "a cook the way she would come home from the market in Nuremberg," with her basket of supplies and a chicken in a net bag. A water tank allowed water to flow into the kitchen through a faucet that could be opened and closed. The kitchen came equipped with tin utensils, and an optional wooden storage box was available. Note that many of the same features are seen in this kitchen, the Folk Art Center's Nuremberg kitchen, and the eighteenth-century print shown below.

In this mid-eighteenth-century print of a full-size German kitchen, the similarities between real and toy kitchens are very evident. Documentation like this image from Colonial Williamsburg's collection enables us to identify the types of utensils that should be included in toy kitchens as well as the appropriate way to display such things as the hanging pans, plates lined up on the shelves, and firewood.

Nuremberg Kitchen

This typical "Nuremberg kitchen" has a central on-hearth cooking area with an overhead flue and wood storage underneath, rows of shelves to display plates, a poultry pen, a checkered pattern on the floor, cutout areas on the shelves for hanging skillets, and a multitude of hooks for pots and pans. These kitchens were so named because Nuremberg was the center of the European toy trade and also be-

Imagine what fun a child would have had lining up these plates and arranging the skillets, numerous sieves, scoops, molds, pots, pans, and even pretend foods in this kitchen. Parents encouraged "cold cooking," which taught children how to organize, measure, and mix ingredients.

cause the toy kitchens resembled real kitchens in South Germany.

The Nuremberg kitchen became popular in the seventeenth century. It remained a popular form into the twentieth century, possibly because children could always add more items to it and possibly because parents placed great importance on miniature kitchens as learning toys.

The Folk Art Center's Nuremberg kitchen is 14 3/4 inches tall by 30 inches wide by 18 3/8 inches deep. Although the inside was repainted many years ago, its unpainted underside and the appearance of what seems to be the original paint on the outside suggest that it was made well before 1900. It cannot be dated by its style alone, since similar Nuremberg kitchens were made over such a long period.

This collection of handcrafted copper was probably made in Europe during the first half of the nineteenth century. Though such items were made in the same manner for many years, making precise dating difficult, the carefully hand-rolled edges, tinned insides, and designs and shapes of these particularly heavy examples suggest an early date of manufacture and Continental origin.

The sieves and strainers found in this toy kitchen were carefully made. Three have nicely rolled edges. The colander in the back right was crafted from especially heavy tinplate.

A meat tenderizer and a tin sieve very similar to ones in the kitchen are shown above in the Märklin catalog of 1895, which stated: "One now begins to realize their [toys'] educational worth." Many German firms manufactured such utensils for toy kitchens during the nineteenth century. Often advertised as "tin," "sheet metal," or "white metal," most of these items were tinplate.

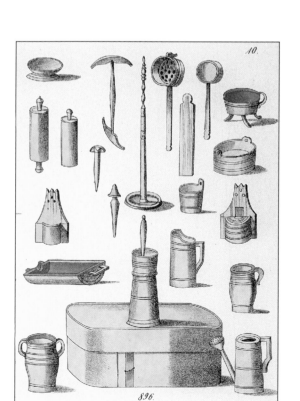

Wooden implements were always found in early kitchens. They were made and exported in great quantities from Germany to England and the United States throughout the eighteenth and nineteenth centuries. Many of the wooden forms found in this kitchen appeared in the Waldkirchen pattern book of about 1850.

The focal point of this toy kitchen is the painted wooden hearth, which in some kitchens was painted to resemble brick or stone with a smoke-stained area on the wall behind it. Wood is laid for a fire under an iron trivet and an eighteenth-century brazier stands nearby. Wooden mixing utensils and a tenderizing mallet are stored beside the hearth in an early nineteenth-century salt-glazed stoneware crock. A large glazed redware Turk's head mold rests on a shelf near several sieves.

A long sheet-iron spatula (or oven peel), a sheet-iron brazier with a turned wooden handle (probably made in Germany about 1780), and a heavy cast-iron waffle iron and kettle represent items spanning many years of manufacture and countless happy hours of play.

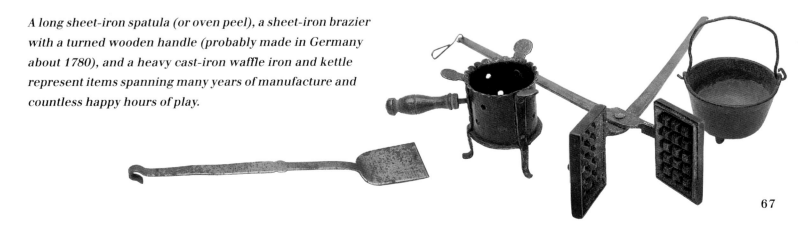

A heavy cast-iron "sad iron," or "smoothing iron," in the shape of a duck and its trivet would have been necessities. (1883 J. & E. Stevens catalog donated for reproduction by Inez B. McClintock.)

ILLUSTRATED CATALOGUE. 45

FANCY DUCK PATTERN

Sad Irons and Stands.

A.	A.	- - -	Length, 1½ in.,	Height 1 in.
	A.	- - -	" 2 "	" 1⅛ "
	B.	- - -	" 2¼ "	" 1¼ "
	C.	- - -	" 2½ "	" 1½ "
	D.	- - -	" 2¾ "	" 1⅝ "
	E.	- - -	" 3¼ "	" 1⅞ "

Several German carved wooden guinea hens and chickens are being kept in a pen and fed from a trough until fattened up. This was a common sight in early kitchens. Doors allowed the birds to be taken in and out of the pens. On the counter above the pen are foods, a duck iron on a trivet, and a variety of tinplate covered spice boxes.

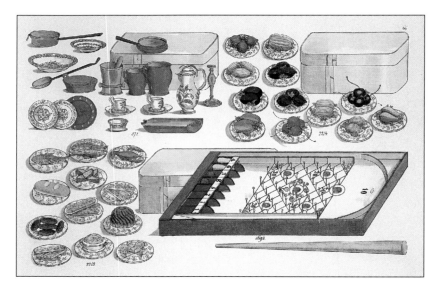

The wooden plates of food on the counter duplicate ones seen in the beautifully hand-colored illustrations of the Waldkirchen pattern book published in Nuremberg about 1850. The examples shown in the pattern book would have been packed for export in "wooden wool," or excelsior, inside wooden packing boxes.

On the right is a sampling of pewter, britannia metal, and pot metal (or pressed-metal) objects. The heavy scalloped pewter dish carries a partial but unidentifiable mark on the bottom. It was probably made in Germany about 1800. The more ornate molded pieces behind it date from the late nineteenth century. This range of wares is typical of those in a kitchen played with over the years, to which both old pieces and new items in "the latest fashion" were added.

A partially opened door reveals china and white graniteware. Pewter plates line the shelves above. The long handles of the brass skillets hang down through triangular holes cut into the shelves. Bread "cools" on a wooden peel and large pots are stored under the shelf.

Item 331 in the Märklin catalog shows the popular tin spoon holder. One hangs to the left. One also is shown on the back wall of the earlier Bestelmeier kitchen on page 64 as well as in the kitchen on page 78.

331   **Löffelbleche,** Weissblech.
Porte-cuillers.
Tin spoon holders.

On the right are two tinplate hinged and lidded boxes, each divided into partitions, and a brass box. Boxes of this type were shown in toy catalogs for herb and spice storage. A similar tinplate spice box from the 1895 Märklin catalog is shown below.

162

Tile-Roof Kitchen

This tile-roof kitchen, probably of German origin, is thought to have been made between 1800 and 1850. The nicely finished details on the exterior are as unusual as its shallow, whitewashed interior. The structure is 23³⁄₄ inches tall, 27¹⁄₈ inches wide, and 13⁷⁄₈ inches deep. It was perhaps intended to be a miniature of an outbuilding with a vented tile roof. Building a kitchen as a separate structure protected a home from kitchen fires, as did the use of tile,

which retarded the spread of fires better than other construction materials. Such a kitchen—either full-size or toy—might have been part of a complex of outbuildings that included stables. The finished sides and hipped roofs of some German stables are similar to this kitchen.

Instead of the more usual division of shelves, small cooking area, and greater depth to the room found in most toy kitchens, here a single cooking surface extends

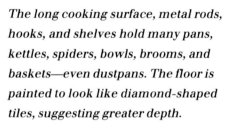

Children were trained to keep their kitchens clean. These brooms and brushes of every size and description were usually sold in sets. Notice the unusual way in which the bristles are tightly laced to hold them in place.

The long cooking surface, metal rods, hooks, and shelves hold many pans, kettles, spiders, bowls, brooms, and baskets—even dustpans. The floor is painted to look like diamond-shaped tiles, suggesting greater depth.

The sides and backs of toy kitchens and shops seldom show such detail. The three-sided hip roof is carved and painted to resemble tile. Its gray pierced chimney is capped by a hip roof. The walls are painted in imitation of brick. The carved cornice, stringcourses, quoining, and foundation are all painted to resemble stone.

the entire length of the room. There is a wide vented hood over the cooking area. The extensive cooking surface of this toy kitchen was probably intended to represent a six-hole "stew" stove for a large household.

Six openings covered by sliding metal doors are built into the front. In full-size kitchens of this design, wood or charcoal fires were built in these spaces and pots were placed over the square holes on the stove's surface. The position of the doors controlled the intensity of the heat. On the back wall behind the iron grate is a smoky area on which the leaping flames of an impressively large wood fire are painted. In the area under the grate is a large opening with a hinged door that probably was an oven or an area in which wood or charcoal was stored. Many utensils are assembled on the shelves and hooks.

This collection of tinplate pieces includes (clockwise from center back): a tall oil lamp with a wick and a saucer to catch drips, a tall coffee filter machine, an oval roasting pan, a bed warmer, a dustpan, a round pan with a built-in soap holder on the right, and a large covered pot with brass handles. A covered storage box is in the center. These are items that every child would have wanted in a kitchen.

ILLUSTRATED CATALOGUE.   57

Skillet.

No. 101, - - - - - - Length, 3¾ in.
No. 101, Porcelain Lined.

Spider.

No. 102, - - - - - - Length, 3½ in.
No. 102, Porcelain Lined.

Kettles.

No. 100, - - - - - Diameter 2 in.
No. 100, Porcelain Lined.
No. 200, - - - - - Diameter, 2½ in.
No. 200, Porcelain Lined.

A page from the 1883 J. & E. Stevens catalog shows three cast-iron utensils similar to those in the toy kitchen. (Catalog donated for reproduction by Inez B. McClintock.)

A closer view shows the flames painted onto the back wall. A door with tin hinges painted black and a latch opens to reveal a baking oven or perhaps storage for wood and charcoal. There are black-painted tin sliding doors on each side of the grate.

Copper kettles and milk pots were popular accessories. Because pots and pans were seldom marked and were made by hand in the same way for many years, it is difficult to date them precisely. An exception is this copper kettle with its pressed and welded curved spout. The kettle's style and method of manufacture indicate it was made about 1850. The pot on the right was probably made earlier.

In addition to the many accessories that hang from every hook and are piled about on the floor, a wooden chopping block and an old wooden bowl with a chopper are convenient to the cooking area. Note the square hole on the surface of the stove and the sliding door below revealing the area where the fire would have been built.

This hollow tin oval "warming-bottle" has a removable brass top with a ring and can be filled with water. It was available in several sizes from the Märklin catalog of 1895. Märklin was one of Germany's largest exporters of metal furnishings, stoves, and toy trains from 1859 until 1959.

No.		
100		**Bettflaschen, rund. Messing.** Bassinoires, rondes, laiton. Brass warming bottles round.
102	Weissblech fer blanc tin Kupfer cuivre poli copper	**Bettflaschen, oval.** Bassinoires, oval. Warming bottles, oval.
104		
105		**Bettflaschen, oval. Zinn.** Bassinoires, oval, en étain poli. Tin founded oval warming-bottles.
106		**Bettflaschen, oval, Zinn mit Becher.** Bassinoires, oval, en étain poli avec gobelet. Tin founded oval warming-bottles with goblet.

No.

Kaffeckannen, Weissblech, konisch, eckig.
244 Cafetières, fer blanc, cannelées.
Tin coffee-pots, fluted form.

Milchkanne, Weissblech, konisch, eckig.
245 Crémiers, fer blanc, cannelées.
Tin milk-pots, fluted form.

Kaffeemaschinen, Weissblech.
249 Cafetières à filtre, fer blanc.
Tin coffee filter machines.

Several forms of coffee- and milk pots similar to those found in this kitchen are seen on this page from the Märklin catalog. Described as "utensils for children's kitchens" in "white metal" or "tin," the pieces were actually cut from thin sheets of iron, welded together, and tin-plated.

Here is another view of the cooking area. In a real kitchen, the whole stove top would have been very hot and would have kept many pots warm when fires burned in the spaces behind the sliding doors. Sieves, colanders, a rolling pin, dustpans, brooms, and several chickens in a pen are all crowded into this area.

In the eighteenth and early nineteenth centuries, poultry was brought home alive and kept in the kitchen in pens or built-in coops until the birds were fattened up and ready for the stewpot.

Turn-of-the-Century Kitchen

Toward the end of the nineteenth century, a new style of toy kitchen that mirrored the changes in real kitchens became popular. A brighter, cleaner look replaced the grimy, sooty appearance found in the older Nuremberg-style kitchens. Several blue and white patterns of lithographed paper imitating delft tiles were used on the walls and floors. White or cream-colored lacquered furniture, which could be scrubbed and kept sparkling clean, was desirable. Metal cookstoves, such as those made by the Märklin firm in Germany or the lead double-eye stove top seen here, were popular.

In this turn-of-the-century German kitchen, which is 13½ inches tall, 26¼ inches wide, and 15½ inches deep, the lacquered furniture is outlined with blue lines, and there are cutout designs on the tops of the glass-doored cabinet, open cupboard, and the "Besenschrank," or broom closet.

The walls of this three-sided kitchen are divided into areas similar to those in a real kitchen of the era, with a chair rail and cornice indicated by narrow patterned lithographed paper borders. The varnish has yellowed, but one can easily imagine the sparkling, clean look this toy kitchen originally had. Notice the meat grinder, chopping block and cleaver, scales, and whisk. A wooden rag box hangs on the wall with a brush resting on its top. Many chores would have been practiced in this toy kitchen.

The broom closet is a special feature whose presence illustrates the importance parents placed on teaching a child to keep a clean and tidy house. Imagine how well trained a child would be with the variety of brushes assembled here! In addition to these cleaning implements, every kitchen had containers of "Soda," "Seife" (soap), and "Sand" for scrubbing not only the walls and floor but also the pots and pans.

This kitchen is unmarked but is very similar to toy kitchens made by the Saxony firm of Moritz Gottschalk from the late nineteenth into the twentieth centuries. In addition to its woodworking shop, the firm also operated its own lithography facility, and some of the papers used in their kitchens are similar to the ones used here. In addition, Gottschalk included such features as the columns painted with blue lines capped with a simple capital similar to the ones seen here.

This corner is filled with items that would have inspired any little girl at the turn of the century to imitate her mother by "cleaning" and "cooking." Every manner of brush and broom as well as "Sand," "Seife" (soap), and "Soda" would help her keep this little room clean. All eleven brooms and brushes can be stored inside the corner cupboard. Notice the blue and white dustpan leaning against the wall.

A tinplate spoon holder, a wire grill, a long-handled strainer, and a ladle hang on the wall above a coffee grinder, double-eye stove top, a rolling pin, and even a small pastry wheel. The much-used coffee grinder's handle still turns and the little drawer at its base pulls out. A child could cut bits of pastry with this little wheel after weighing her flour and rolling the dough with the rolling pin.

Two sets of blue and white glazed ceramic canisters (one set for sago, coffee, semolina, sugar, rice, and barley, the other for almonds, cinnamon, pepper, and nutmeg) line two shelves. Three "Exceline-Nickel" soup tureens or pots are lined up on the shelf.

410 | **Suppenschüsseln mit Decke**
Terrines, fer blanc.
Tin soup terrines.

A tin soup tureen shown in the 1895 Märklin catalog is similar to the three pots on the open shelves above.

This small shop is 8 inches tall by 13 inches wide by 8 inches deep. Its exterior is painted blue-green with yellow accents. The interior trim is also blue-green, but the counter, the twenty-four drawers, and the floor are stained a reddish brown. Each drawer was made individually and fits in its own particular spot. The inscription on the sign is painted on paper that is glued onto the front roof crest.

Dry Goods Shop

This small late nineteenth-century German dry goods shop advertises its wares—"Material Handlung"—in white Old Gothic letters on the wooden crest over the front. Two half-round columns have been applied to each of the front sections. An opening is created by a divided counter.

There are three vertical rows of drawers with a series of arched openings underneath on each of the three walls.

What fun a child would have playing with this store. The young shopkeeper would learn pricing, stocking, packaging, and perhaps how to keep accounts.

The cubbyholes are filled with lace, bolts of fabric, sample cards, pins, threads, and other goods one would expect to find in such a shop. A child proprietor could fill the drawers with all sorts of small treasures. Two tiny peg-wooden dolls (one in an egg), a cast-iron "smoothing iron," and some skeins of threads are displayed on the counter.

The style of painting on the sides of the shop and between the two half-round applied columns on each side of the front indicates its place and date of manufacture as the Erzgebirge region of Germany in the 1880s. How reminiscent the decoration is of the Noah's arks made in that area: the painted and shaded quoins on the corners; the design, colors, and proportions of the windows; and the band of color at the base. The most outstanding similarity is the painted floral frieze across the top of each side.

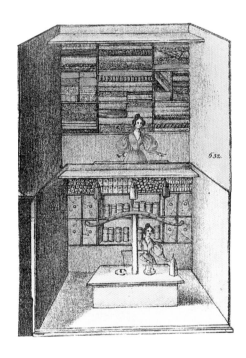

Three shops from German toy catalogs are shown. On the left are two small dry goods shops from about 1840 by the Sonneberg firm of Louis and Edward Lindner. Above is a sweets, spice, and dry goods shop from a Nuremberg pattern book from around 1850–1860.

Millinery Shop

The shelves of this nineteenth-century German millinery shop are filled with laces, beading, nets, fabrics, flowers, chains, ribbons, other trims, and hatboxes. Along the top shelf are eleven milliner's mannequins modeling fashionable and beautifully made hats.

The interior walls and top two shelves are painted pink with light blue facings. The counter is painted cream with dark blue lines and a rose border. A velvet ribbon encircles the counter's base. Perhaps drawers would have gone into the unpainted sections, as seen in the dry goods shop on pages 80–81.

The gold dressing table, gold clock (marked "patented Nov. 28, '76—Arthur E. Hotchkis"), and silver chair (marked "patented Aug. 18, '69") may have been added by a child-owner. A Sonneberg doll from the 1820s is dressed in a pale pink dress and hat. Her arms and legs are carved from wood and she has a composition head and shoulders.

Though few miniature rooms of this period have a signature or mark, a printed paper label on the bottom shows the intertwined initials "CH" in a shield surmounted by a crown and the word "Schutzmarke" signifying a protected trademark. Christian Hacker headed a firm of toy makers founded in Nuremberg in 1870. This par-

These mannequins are painted in the manner of early nineteenth-century peg-wooden dolls with thin brows, rosy cheeks, red lips, and dark eyes. Note how the hairstyles vary.

Both the shop, which is 9 1/8 inches tall by 21 3/4 inches wide by 8 1/2 inches deep, and the mannequins are made of painted soft pine. Some areas show considerable wear, but these signs of use cannot hide the beauty of the dolls' painted faces or the workmanship of the hats, the tiny drawstring reticule, the minute monogrammed handkerchief, or the paper-covered hatboxes.

ticular mark was used by the firm from 1875 into the early twentieth century. Though the interior of the shop has been repainted, the exterior shows Hacker's characteristic cream background painting and fine dark lines tracing the outline of the left side section. This section has a lithograph of a seated man being served a drink by a black man behind a bar. This scene and the repainted interior suggest that this room originally was a different kind of shop.

The hats the mannequins are modeling and the mannequins themselves also present a puzzle. While the shop dates no earlier than 1875, the most modern of the hats is in a style popular no later than 1850,

and the style of the painting and details of the faces of the mannequins suggest the period 1820 to 1840. Perhaps the collection of mannequins and their hats was put into this worn structure in more recent times, maybe the shop's young owner was intrigued by doll clothes from an earlier era, or perhaps the hats and mannequins were handed down to a child who had just received a new toy shop.

Enigmas often occur when a much-enjoyed structure is filled and played with by several children or generations of children. We can only imagine what might have been the actual story behind a puzzling combination of items.

Toy Post Office

During the second half of the nineteenth century, many new kinds of toys intended to stimulate a child's imagination became popular. This post office could have occupied a group of children who took turns playing the postmaster or postmistress sorting and distributing the mail while others were the customers mailing or picking up letters. The post office is hand-painted and was made in part from a wooden packing box.

The post office is very similar to one advertised as an "entirely new and original toy" in Carl P. Stirn's 1893 catalog. With the advent of quicker and more reliable steamship and railroad travel, importers like Stirn could offer a greater variety of toys in wider price ranges. In addition to introducing "new and original" toys, Stirn assured his customers that "since 1875 I have visited the European markets regularly and arranged for the manufacture of all the goods imported by the old firm [of Stirn and Lyon]."

The hand-painted toy post office at the Folk Art Center is constructed of pine and glass. It is almost the same size (19 inches tall by 23 1/2 wide by 4 inches deep) as the lithographed example in the Stirn catalog and appears to have been copied from the catalog or a very similar example.

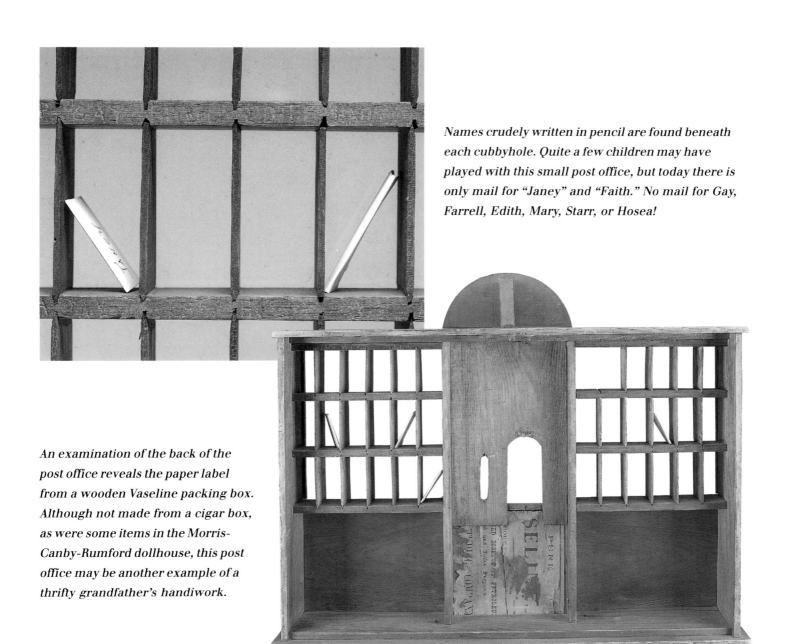

Names crudely written in pencil are found beneath each cubbyhole. Quite a few children may have played with this small post office, but today there is only mail for "Janey" and "Faith." No mail for Gay, Farrell, Edith, Mary, Starr, or Hosea!

An examination of the back of the post office reveals the paper label from a wooden Vaseline packing box. Although not made from a cigar box, as were some items in the Morris-Canby-Rumford dollhouse, this post office may be another example of a thrifty grandfather's handiwork.

No. 48. U. S. POST OFFICE.

An entirely new and original toy, affording children a most pleasing and instructive entertainment. Ten each of Toy Postal Cards and envelopes accompany P. O. It is elaborately lithographed and ornamented in handsome style and colors, has glass front and 56 letter boxes, is strongly made, and comes nearly set up. Each one carefully packed in a box. Size, 23 inches long, 19 inches high.

Price, per dozen. $8.50

This toy post office shown in Carl Stirn's Illustrated Fall and Holiday Catalogs of Foreign and Domestic Dolls, Toys, and Games *(New York, 1893) is an example of the widespread use of lithography in dollhouses, shops, and kitchens and also in furnishings.*

Acknowledgments

Many people have contributed to the production of this book and I gratefully acknowledge their help:

To Carolyn Weekley, the director of the Abby Aldrich Rockefeller Folk Art Center, who encouraged a book on the dollhouses in response to the requests of many visitors. Her suggestion has opened exciting new areas for future research.

To Anne Motley for her careful monitoring during the photography of the many relocations of the objects.

To the staff at the Folk Art Center, particularly Debbie Green, Pat Bedtelyon, Osborne Taylor, Sr., James Parker, Gethsemane Gallop, and the security staff for their help during photography.

To Tom Green for his skill in bringing to life these dollhouses, toy kitchens, shops, and their contents. His sensitive photography of small vignettes and his willingness to find the best angle and lighting allow the details of the design and texture of special small objects to be shown. Tom was ably assisted by Lael White.

To Trix Rumford and her family for their interest and help in providing information, photographs, young nieces, a nephew—and even the chair that was "always used" by the children when they played with the wonderful dollhouse. Her careful review of the manuscript was also appreciated.

To Suzanne Coffman for her skillful editing of the manuscript.

To Helen Mageras for her handsome design for this book, which does justice to these structures and to the many interesting small details.

To Colonial Williamsburg's curators and historians who turned their attention from large scale to small scale: Barbara Luck, John Davis, Ron Hurst, Betty Leviner, Linda Baumgarten, Janine Skerry, Margaret Pritchard, John Austin (retired), and Carl Lounsbury.

To the staffs of the library and outreach productions, who are always helpful in locating sources and images and in processing film on a tight schedule: Liz Ackert, Del Moore, Mary Keeling, Laura Arnette, Cathy Grosfils, Mary Norment, and Kathy Dunn.

To friends in the community for their help and encouragement, including Diane Spence for help with special setups, Terry Meyers for help with searching the Internet, and Hildegärd Dimmert and Peter Jesse for their translations of German nineteenth-century toy catalogs, correspondence, and publications.

To volunteers Ken Spoor, who kindly helped with the procurement of rare books and catalogs, and Ralee Durden, Leslie Johnson, and Colleen Brush, who assisted with illustrations and marketing research.

To friends at other museums and miniature associations and collectors for their help and encouragement, especially Flora Gill Jacobs, the Washington Dolls' House and Toy Museum; Ellen Manyon and Carol Sandler, The Strong Museum; Margaret Bleecker Blades, Chester County Historical Society; Mary Wheeler, Toy and Miniature Museum of Kansas City; Bob Grew, Tom McCandless, and Inez McClintock of the Antique Toy Collectors of America; Virginia Merrill; and Lorraine May Punchard.

And finally a very special thanks to the many donors whose gifts have enriched the collection and have provided pleasure for the visitors to the museum, and to the many volunteers who over the years have helped with the dollhouses. They have carefully installed the objects, polished silver, ironed curtains, refurbished dried flowers, and made foods each Christmas and all too soon packed everything away with care for the next year.

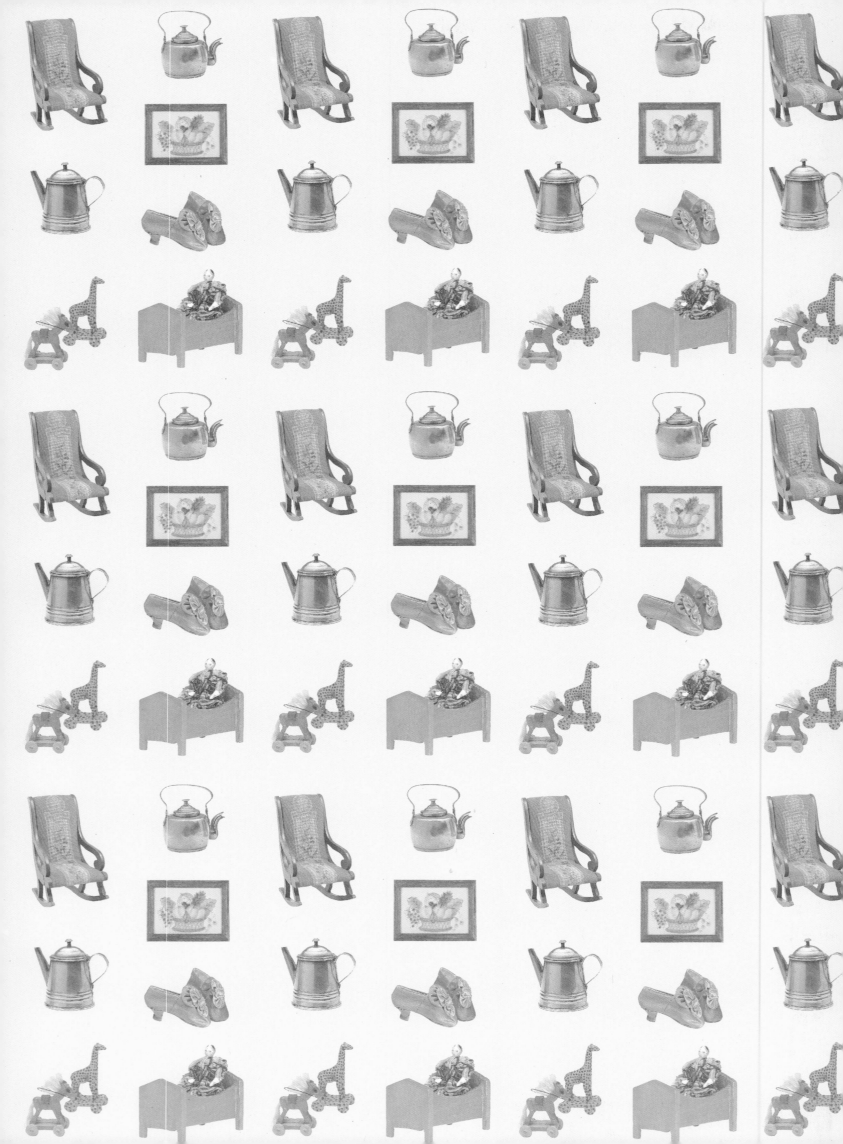